HITCHED PUBLISHING

WOBBLY

A twenty-something-year-old's perspective on life.

Beth Hitchman's honest, vulnerable and unique perspective on life expressed through verse. Her candour is inspiring and refreshing. Beth deliberately pushes the boundaries and challenges the rules in life and in poetry.

by Beth Hitchman

Wobbly
A twenty-something-year-old's perspective on life.

Copyright © 2018 by Beth Hitchman
Editor: Lainey Hitchman
Illustrated by Lainey Hitchman

All rights reserved. No part of this book may be reproduced in any form by any electronic or mechanical means including photocopying, recording, or information storage and retrieval without permission in writing from the author.

ISBN: 9781911176060
Book Website
www.redrabble.com
Email:redrabblepoetry@gmail.com

WOBBLY
A twenty-something-year-old's perspective on life.

A collection of poems
by Beth Hitchman

ACKNOWLEDGEMENTS

To everyone I wrote a poem for.

To everyone that told me I should write.

To everyone that told me I should write a book.

Contents

ACKNOWLEDGEMENTS   iv

LOVE AND OTHER MISTAKES I'VE MADE   1

You	2
Contact	2
Dawn	3
Lost Cause	3
Bad For Me	4
Past	4
Drifting	5
Missed	6
Hers	6
I'm Fine Here	7
When He Looks At You	8
Plaster	9
To The Boy I Chose	10
I Wish You Well	11
I Lose	12
The Escape	13
Young Dumb Love	14

MY BEST ATTEMPT AT CHANGING THE WORLD ONE POEM AT A TIME   15

Time Machine	16

Decomposition	18
Thin Air	19
I'm Human Too	20
Life Is Too Short	22
Dog	23
To The Loved Ones Who Do Not Know That They Are Loved	24
In The Making And Breaking	26
Splatters	28
The Givers	29
SELF-DISCOVERY AND OTHER ADVENTURES	**30**
Dream World	31
Me	31
The Dancer	32
Travelling	33
Perspective	34
The Song	34
Commitment	35
The Paragraph Poem	36
Version of Me	38
Mirror	40
Essence	40
OTHER EMOTIONS I STRUGGLE TO EXPRESS	**41**
Sad	42

Big Fish	42
The Time Travelling Of A Wanderer	43
Breaking Walls	44
Regeneration	46
White Noise	47
The Block	48
Car Crash	48
Phobia	49
Responsibility	49
Condition	50
Through My Window	51
Meadow	52
Worthy	53
AUTHOR BIO	55

LOVE AND OTHER MISTAKES I'VE MADE

You

I lie awake, and think of anything but you...
I cannot think, of anything but you.
I watch a movie, and the love I see is you.
I read a book, and scrawled across the pages...
Is you.

Contact

Vacant stares,
Ill-prepared,
Fingers run
Through stray hairs,
City streets,
Strangers you meet,
Stuck in lives,
Left on repeat.

Dawn

You were a shadow.
You followed me across countries,
You followed me across books,
You lost yourself: in simple lies,
In oceans, rivers and brooks.

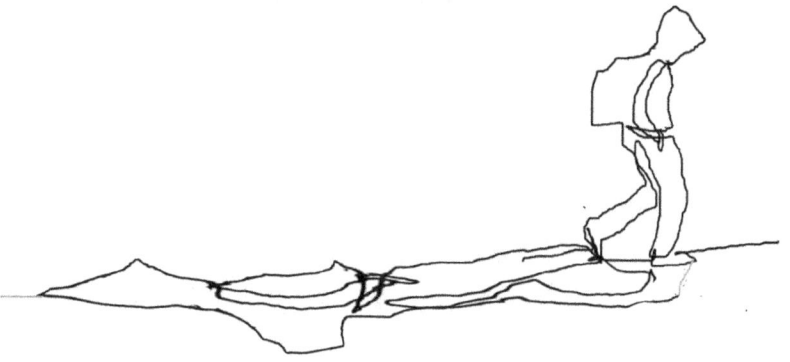

Lost Cause

They don't feel that way;
You don't think they ever will,
You feel lost again.

Bad For Me

You are like a sledgehammer to the heart,
Every time I try to say your name,
Every time I try to say hello,
I can't do this anymore.
I have used you as an ideal,
As a fantasy… it isn't working!

Past

Sent me music,
Wrote me songs.

Lyrics weren't right,
Sounds were wrong.

Lost in melody,
Left to forget.

Love went lonely,
No one else was left.

Drifting

You make me feel like I cannot breathe.
Like I am twisting underwater...
Unable to sink or swim,
Simply floating.

This is the way a decisive heart feels:
It feels lost,
It feels lonely,
It feels oh so happy when you smile.

It's been so long
since I've seen you smile,
I have missed you...
I don't want to drift alone anymore.

Missed

I still think of you,
I am lost and lonely,
I am a walking contradiction
... I am still yours.

Hers

Get over it, get over it!
My brain screams in despair.

It could never happen anyway,
To her I can't compare.

She who stole your heart away,
The one I haven't met.

I invested so much time in you,
Time only she will get.

I'm Fine Here

You haunt me.
My lines are lost
I loosen my lips
No sound comes out.

You lost me.
You left me here
I cannot leave
I wait for you.

You left me.
I no longer fear
The standing still
I'm fine here.

I am strong.
Not left alone
But standing still
I'm fine here.

When He Looks At You

When he looks at you,
You are so aware...
Of every move you make,
Trying to portray beauty,
In every step you take.
This is what it is like to fall in love,
To be infatuated with someone,
To imagine fingers intertwined,
To want to write a love poem,
Even after the battle scars...
I have learnt to feel again.

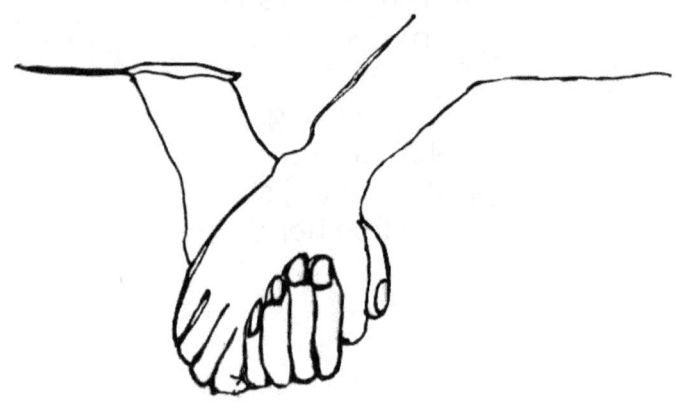

Plaster

Tearing me away from you,
Like a plaster.
Slowly and surely...
So we both feel the pain,
For a prolonged period of time.

This way you won't forget me,
This way I won't forget you...
You don't know why I am doing this yet,
You feel hurt and confused.
I smile sadly at the pain I have caused.

But, doing this might help you
Say goodbye more easily.
Doing this might mean you'll love me less.
Doing this might mean you'll become happier.
Doing this means you'll be fine once I have left.

I will be remembered as a splatter on the wall;
Leaving stains like decorations,
And hoping you won't repaint.
I know you will remember me,
So I will remember you.

To The Boy I Chose

To the boy I chose to love:
You are not a boy,
Not any more.
You never seemed to fit
The mould of man,
But perhaps that's exactly why
I viewed you as my friend.

You told me you loved me;
From the very first awkward mishap.
I can't seem to accept that,
I accused you
Of getting attached too quickly,
But when you said that; my heart leapt,
How contradicting!

You are my first great decision!
Because I chose you,
You didn't just happen.
You gave me time to think.
I didn't fall, I calculated.
Granted I chose wrong
And hurt us both.

At least we felt that pain.
I cannot pretend I didn't enjoy us.
While it lasted, It was beautiful,
But beauty never lasts,
And ours was bound to fail.
Now, all we have are memories,
At least we have our memories.

I Wish You Well

The minute
I do well,
Is the hour
I fall.
For the sake
of a love,
Which means
nothing at all!
I'm splitting
myself,
From my body
as of now.
I'm not running
my darling,
I'm taking
my final bow!

I Lose

I wish the way,
You walked over my shoulders,
Would hurt less...
If I were stronger,
Maybe I could've held you...
Supported you and kept you going.
As it is you are leaning,
On someone else's body.
I'm left sprawled out on the floor,
With a lot less pressure;
Still feeling like I failed you.
The sting of weight on my back,
Where I once felt you,
Reminds me how hard it is to suck in air...
When your ribs are forced to the floor.
I can't move!
You win.

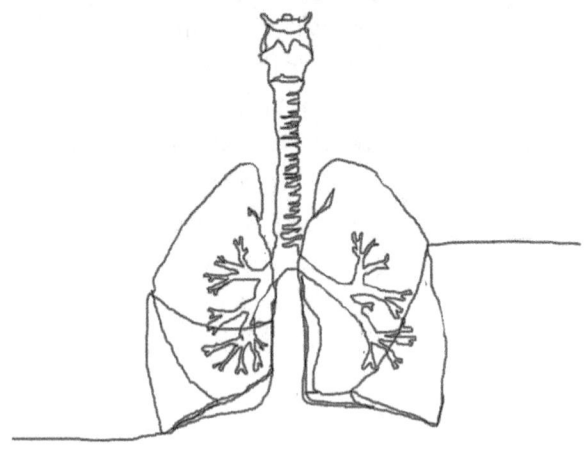

The Escape

I ran so fast
I swear the wind swooshed!
I don't know what you expected
When you told me it wasn't safe,
But it probably wasn't that.
I came back not to let you protect me;
I'm here to tell you I don't regret it.
I never looked back.
You are the sun, she is the moon,
And I am the backwards meteor!

Hurtling as fast as I can away
From anything that pulls me...
Head so filled up with stories,
It aches when I don't write.
Dreams I can never remember,
Still keep me awake at night.
I wanted to tell you,
I no longer need your arms,
Wrapped so tightly around me...
You can let go now.

Young Dumb Love

You, you make me smile stupid.
Smile, as I imagine your lips melting onto mine,
I imagine folding into your arms,
Moulding my arms to fit into the nook of your back.
I see myself on your shoulders,
My hair tied up in a ponytail,
Reaching for the leaves on a tree,
Doing childish things.
Because love is young and dumb,
And that's all I ever want to be.

MY BEST ATTEMPT AT CHANGING THE WORLD ONE POEM AT A TIME

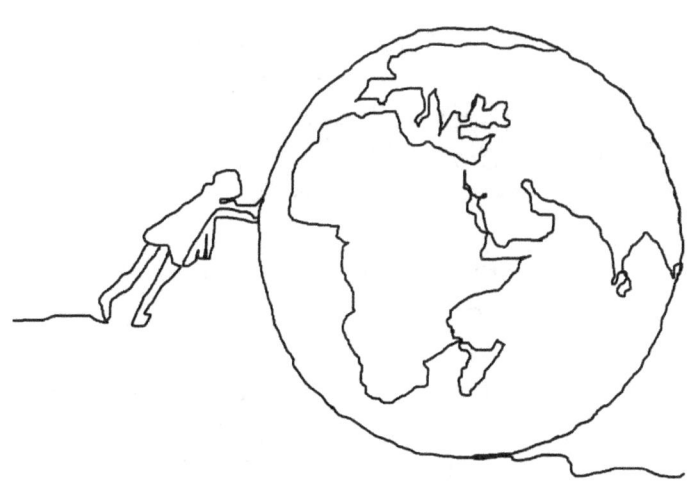

Time Machine

I am a living time machine.

Ask me to tell you a story,
I will take you back in time,

Repeat it until it's boring...
Until you know the story
Like the back of your hand.

The same old words,
The same old dance,
Lost in the woods
Without a chance.

This is how I tell my story.
Once upon a time,
There was a little girl,
She couldn't write,
She couldn't rhyme.

That's all she ever wanted.
Words that haunted.
That made people understand,
The tragedy of losing self-expression.
Confused and hurt,
By failure and oppression...

This is the warning of the time machine.
Never tell a little child
That they can't do anything.
Because children will listen.
At the very worst of times.
When you lose your patience,
When you're at the end of the line.

Children will listen,

They'll believe what you say.

They'll repeat that boring story,

Until the end of day.

Decomposition

Cover your compost!
It will stop the flies from getting at it...
Does it matter if the flies eat it?
It is all rotting anyway...
Bring it out into the open,
Ask people to stop and stare...
They will find it offensive!
You will be asked to remove it,
Cover your compost!

Thin Air

As our words scream out in anger,
Our thoughts are disengaged,
Our hearts begin to falter,
As they feel the others pain.

A wrath that shouldn't be felt,
By the one that they adore,
The fire in their eyes,
As they kick open the door.

The saddened loosened fingers,
To that white door grasp and cling,
The fragile heart of their beloved,
No more joy allowed to bring.

Hazel eyes so lonely,
Feeling nothing but despair,
Wondering, waiting, watching,
Staring into nothing but thin air.

The past that was forgiven,
Is the burden that she bears,
As people loving her realise,
The lies hidden behind golden hair.

I'm Human Too

I will not wear my heart
On the edge of my sleeve...
Unless you ask me to.
This way I will never
Have to inconvenience anyone.
With explaining why
I don't feel like smiling...
I will only talk if they ask.

Fortunately for me,
It is usually a statement.
"Smile! You look prettier
When you're happy!"
How condescending they can be
Always manages to surprise me.
I will not tell them my secret,
not even one of these.

I might not seem
Like a human to you,
But extroverts do not
Understand me anyway...
Understand, I do not hate you.
When I say no to going out
It's because I'm probably,
Wrapped up in a book.

Social outings
Make me uncomfortable,
In fact, so do
Social anythings...
Talking is not my strong point.
I do not have the talent;
Of thinking
Before I speak.

Understand I don't blame you,
For not understanding...
I don't understand how dancing,
In a crowded room
Would beat candles,
A bubble bath,
And a brand new adventure.
But understand I accept you.

I would appreciate the same.

Life Is Too Short

Arrogance will never
Get you anywhere my child,
Neither will your moaning.
I hear your voice rattling,
Your blood turning black,
You will not give me a chance,
To squeeze in the hope of yellow.

You and I just met today,
Already you have my pity...
Not because you sold me your story,
But because you allowed me to realise
You will always be like this.

You feel like the world
Owes you something!
That is a dangerous thought to own.
You feel as if you're
Walking on an edge,
As if the void is waiting
To swallow you whole.
When really, it just wants you to go home...

You are safe now,
Life will get you in the end,
You shouldn't dwell on its attempts,
Life is too short to feel sorry for yourself.
Life is too short!

Dog

You cannot fear a dog's bite,
If you remove its teeth.

You cannot fear it,
Without its claws,
Without its tongue.

Now you have a dog that cannot speak,
Now you have a dog that cannot eat.

To The Loved Ones Who Do Not Know That They Are Loved

You, my darling,
Have small hands,
And big eyes.
Your tears
Are far too big,
For your hands
To ever catch.
Which is why
You feel like
You're drowning,
Every time you cry.
You don't have
To push your hands
To your face like that...
They won't help
The tears disappear
Into your skin.
My darling, tears
Are not a bad thing.
There is no shame in them.
You do not have to hide
Them from me.
If you were bleeding,
I would get you a plaster.

Now you are crying,
I will get you a tissue.
You don't have to stand,
Alone and lost...
I will come find you,
We can be lost together.
So take these words
Like a letter, and know
That I will always hide
From humanity with you.
People are scary
But don't always
Be afraid of them.
Some will be there to catch you,
Even before you start to fall.

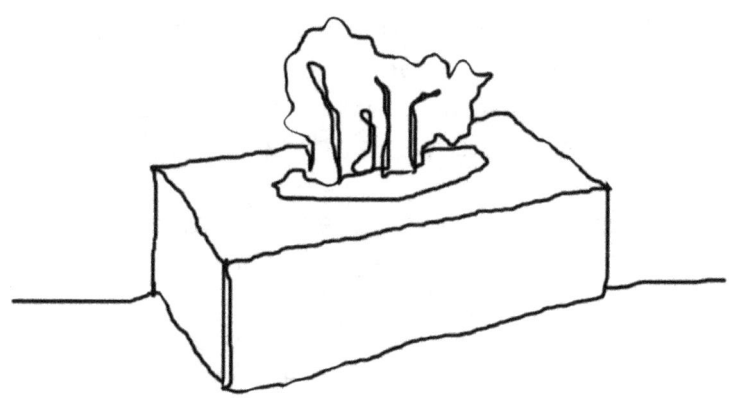

In The Making And Breaking

Have you ever felt unappreciated,
And desperately alone,
Your friends love and support you,
But you're a stranger in your own home.

A depth of insecurity,
You question your own techniques,
Everything you've ever learnt,
Undermined for a bit of peace.

Opinions and lessons that should be heard,
Because so much can be implied.
A child so fragile and new to life,
Can easily have their dreams denied.

Lack of knowledge and character,
Is a terrifyingly real threat.
You say he's only a child,
But that's just for now.
Do you really want to take that bet?

The way you raise a child,
Is how they will live.
Your influence and life lessons,
Is all you'll ever give.

So think carefully when letting go,
Of intelligent punishment.
It's not just the child, but the child's growth,
That deserves more than your sweet sentiment!

Splatters

You think you can do what you want,
Just because your life was better,
Than the fewer
And the seekers
And the believers.
What if I told you that
You were no more loved,
Than the shadows,
And the splatters,
And everything else
That should matter?
No amount of forgiveness
Can change trust that you've broken.
Different words can be spoken,
But my dreams are torn open.
So when you tell me
What you would like to see in the world,
Take hold of your vision
Instead of just sitting and waiting,
For someone else to realise
The truth you have discovered.
Don't tell me you can't be bothered.
Your passion has been ignited
Why are you trying to fight it?

The Givers

"I want to become the earth one day,
I want to get around."
Declared the young girl merrily,
Hands sunk into the ground.
"And why is that?"
Replied the boy,
"Don't you want to live?"
"No, I don't" answered the girl,
"It's life I want to give."

SELF-DISCOVERY AND OTHER ADVENTURES

Dream World

I wish you would,
Or, I wish I could.
Then you could be with me.
I'd hold you close,
And snuggle up,
Then have a cup of tea.

Me

I don't have to be the best,
As long as I am me.
I've been blinded for so long,
How did I never see?

The Dancer

I lost my voice,
While tapping my toes.
Where it went to,
Nobody knows.

Distractions come,
Distractions go,
Where my voice went to,
Nobody knows.

My feet they dance,
My hips they sway,
When I had my voice,
They never moved that way.

When I wasn't happy,
I used to write,
I think I dance now,
Because I finally feel alright.

Travelling

I don't like boats,
I cannot cope,
With how they float,
I don't like boats.

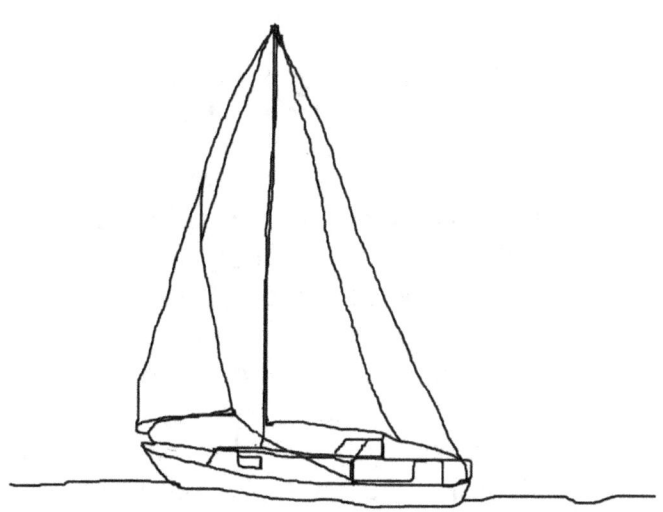

Perspective

Fall back.
Find yourself.
Trust somebody.
Steal away some time.
Go for a walk in a garden.
Let yourself be honest.
Let yourself feel.
Don't panic.
It's okay.

The Song

I found perfection in my poetry,
I found a way to express myself.
I do not play an instrument,
Still you have me trying,
To use my voice a different way.
The song you will never hear
Basically says...
In a beaten-bush roundabout fashion,
That I like the way you like me,
And I hope you will stay.

Commitment

Open your eyes,
I wish you could see me.
I want you to hear me
What I long to say,
But I'm afraid.
You know my habits and hobbies,
And I know yours but...
I'm not sure I like this story.
The pages force themselves to turn,
I am not allowed to stop,
Or even to slow them.
The best I can do is hope
You never get brave,
That the question will never come,
Because when it flies from your lips,
I will be forced to run.

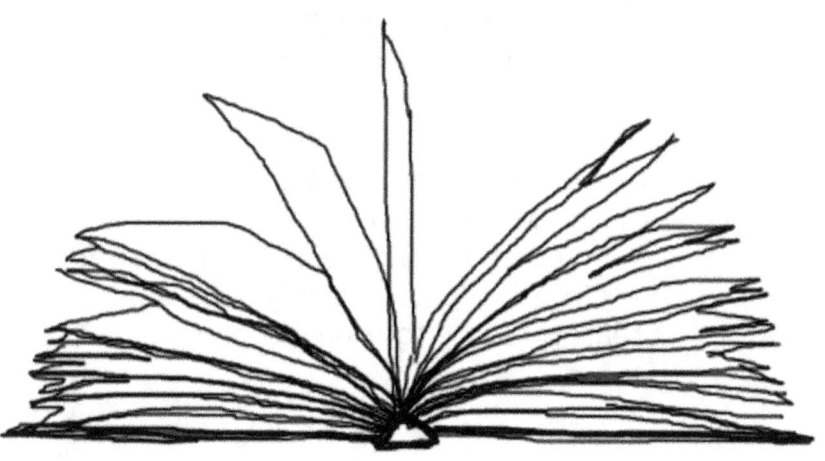

The Paragraph Poem

What if I just wrote? Wrote letters to form words and words to form sentences. What if I found the perfect combination between poetry and paragraphs?

What if I wrote and was read?
What if I wrote and was published?
What if I wrote and was understood?
What if I spoke?

What if I spoke what was written while biting my lip and sitting with an old guitar singing my poems? Then I would be considered an artist! Why should I change? I don't want to be a singer, I want to be a writer and a thinker and a bringer.

What if I cried?
Well, that would make me pathetic!
What if I died?
Well, that would make it poetic.

What if I let rage deep down in my soul? Well, then I'd grow bitter and old, living all on my own in my twenties. I'd be a recluse, let loose by the maniacs that must've been special and died. That could be the only possible reason for my sorrow and pride.

But I am just me,
Little old me,
Writing what I want...
Happy as can be.

To everyone, it seems that I am happy because my life was easy, or so they think. Just because I don't show that I have been to the brink of hell and back doesn't mean that I haven't received a bit more than a slap.

I keep it a secret,
Dress it up in ribbons and bows,
It must mean that I am happy...
But why should I be happy?

People have given up for a lot less than what I've been through; maybe you should look before you think that I am see-through. The brightness of life is what I choose to look like, so that there is hope.

I dress up with ribbons and smile like the sun...
My choice, not yours, to show life that I've won!
My depths are filled with sorrow and pain,
But my highs, like the sun,
You'll always see them again.

Version of Me

I am who I am,
Which is every part of me.
I am the dumb, the smart,
And everything in between.

I am the table that's been turned,
I am a friend who tries true.
I am so many lessons learned,
I still have to learn a few.

An unsurpassable amount,
Of words to define me.
I am undefinable,
I am what nobody can see.

I am dreams,
I am alone at night.
I have my own plans,
I am afraid to bring to light.

I am a defenceless woman.
I am a battle breaking down.
I am re-opened scars
A smile-stitched frown.

A light nobody's seen,
Has just caught
Glimpses of...
The real me.

The undefinable, understandable,
Irrational, conventional,
Fantastical, nonsensical,
Version of me.

Mirror

I only realise it is bad,
When I am so tired,
I take a deep breath,
And feel my lungs shatter.

Essence

This my darling is a lifestyle...
We go boom!
Girls like me do grow on sugar plum trees,
But we are made of a little bit more,
Than sugar or fruit.
We have a special x,
That makes people go mute.
I can't see the light that controls the flame,
So I'll decide to make my own,
And then...
I'll go...
Boom!

OTHER EMOTIONS I STRUGGLE TO EXPRESS

Sad

I'm sad right now,
I don't know why,
All I seem to do is cry.

Some say it's work,
Some say it's me,
Others say it's in between.

Big Fish

You stick out like a sore thumb,
You're the one they like to tease.
You've never had a date because,
All you want to do is leave.
This town is too small
For a talent like yours.
So you set out to find
A bigger city to conquer.
With thousands of floors
And billions of doors.

The Time Travelling Of A Wanderer

I feel like a thousand days,
I don't even know what that means.
I'm lost floating somewhere confused,
By lives and times and in-betweens.

I could sail away on adventures,
I could stay at home with tea.
I could go out on a wandering way,
Or leave the wanderers be.

I could ride a train to nowhere,
I could lose myself in a book.
I could discover a brand new island,
Or bring a story to my reading nook.

I could find a beautiful scene,
I could go on a walk 'round my block.
I could climb and dive and never come back...
Or I could sit, swing my legs, watch the clock.

Breaking Walls

I know it's been too long since
I've written an honest poem.
When I sit down to write I feel nervous.
I'm so used to using metaphors,
That I've forgotten the first reason
I love poetry...

If I was less focused on making sure
I put up a wall between me
And whomever I wish to affect,
Maybe I would be able to do
What I wished in the first place.

If I cared less about whether
Or not this rhymed or had structure.
Perhaps I would hit something hard
Instead of tiptoeing around those walls;
That were created to be broken.

I was never created to be soft and silent,
These walls were never formed
to remain unbent.
I won't forget what my teacher told me,
"Learn the rules like a pro,
So you can break them like an artist."

I am not claiming to be a pro in any way,
Or even an artist. Let's make that clear.

But if I hope to make it one day,
I had better start acting like I am.
I will not short list my work any more!
No more calling them, "Silly little poems".
When people ask me what I do
in my spare time,
I will simply reply...

'Poetry'.

I bare my soul on lined notebooks until I feel relief.

'Poetry'!

Regeneration

I am pulling myself
Away from people.

Too close,
Too close.

Keep them at arm's length.
I find myself hiding in my room.

Reading and writing,
Unable to bear the outside world.

I fear that if I have to be social,
I will crack...

Let me regather my strength,
Or I will crack!

This is not an observation,
This is a threat!

I will
Crack!

White Noise

Fear is crippling...
Hello, old friend.

I have felt this
Feeling many times.
Now the urge to run,
Overwhelms me again.

How do I fight
Without energy?
How do I focus,
When the world grips my attention.

I don't know where to look,
How does one focus
In this mass of white noise?
In this silencing white noise.

Hello, old friend.

The Block

Emotionally drained...
Nit-picking my thoughts,
'Til there is nothing left in my brain.
Overtired, with a massive headache,
Wanting to write,
Realising there is nothing to say.

Car Crash

I learnt today,
That it doesn't have to be you
That gets hit by the car.
Sometimes you still feel the pain,
Especially when hospitals
Pull you apart.

Phobia

Afraid of heights but you've never fallen.
You go on each day to keep the ball rolling.
Afraid of living but afraid to die.
Afraid to question or even answer the why,
"Who?" is the question you don't understand,
Who will help on the road you have planned.
A deep dark secret that nobody knows,
Before you tell, figure out who to show.

Responsibility

We lost ourselves in the fire,
Cause we couldn't see through the smoke,
We didn't know the way out,
Because we didn't listen to good folk,
We lost ourselves in the temper,
Because we couldn't control ours,
We learnt from you our leader,
So the blood on your hands is ours.

Condition

I have no grammatical structure.
Words do not flow out of me,
Not without my stutter.
I find it hard to catch my breath.
Simple ideas steal it away,
Until there is nothing left,
But my faint heart beating-
Beating inside my chest.

I go to the left,
Because nothing is right,
Not since the theft,
That came in the night.
I claim individuality,
Because of this,
Just like everybody else.
Hurt, like everybody else.

This broke into my soul,
Captured my heart,
Accelerated the old.
Created the new me
That suffered from:
Pain and abuse,
Hurt in the heart,
Lost and confused.

Started on fuel.
Young enough to
Still drink fruit juice...

Through My Window

Green
Leaves,
Red berry
Bushes,
Open
Windows,
Clanging
Of dishes,
The sound
Of music,
Floating through
The air,
Sunlight on the
Mossy roof,
Whistling
Without a care.

Meadow

This is the field where the wild things grow,
They call them flowers but nobody knows,
That they are made of dreams, nightmares and hopes,
This is the field where the wild things grow.

This is the field where the wild things grow,
What's in the soil nobody knows,
But it creates the most beautiful show,
This is the field where the wild things grow.

This is the field where the wild things grow,
Where children play in rain or snow,
And visions are given as they lie in the grass,
This is the field where the wild things last.

Worthy

Who told you,
'You're not worthy',
Of what you hold dear?

Who told you,
'You can't'?
Who taught you to fear?

Who told you,
'You're nothing'?
They don't have a clue,

This is my advice to you
Do exactly the opposite of
Whatever they say.

Then one day,
You'll be standing,
And they all will see,

You challenged,
The idea of who they
thought you would be.

AUTHOR BIO

Beth Hitchman is a chef turned call-centre worker, turned "actually I want to go to university and study English Literature and creative writing" student.

She fills her time with home renovation, fighting the plants in her garden and writing poetry. Beth has performed several of her spoken word poems at meetings and events.

If you want to read more then visit her website redrabble.com for blog posts and book updates.

www.ingramcontent.com/pod-product-compliance
Lightning Source LLC
Chambersburg PA
CBHW071320080526
44587CB00018B/3303